I0476574

Table of Contents

Introduction

Welcome and thank you for purchasing my book, *Kindle Publishing Unveiled - How to Write, Upload And Sell Your Book..*

Kindle Direct Publishing, or KDP, is a section from Amazon which allows *anyone* to publish an eBook and to make money online.

By going through this quick start guide, you will understand what it takes to write, sell, market, and generate passive income.

Now, let's get started.

Chapter 1: Why KDP?

I'm glad you asked.

Amazon is one of the biggest online retailers and it has an enormous potential in regard to online selling and marketing (physical products, books, etc.). For those who want to start an online business using this powerful engine, things might get interesting as time goes by.

What makes the difference?

When people are searching for something on Google, they don't necessarily look for something to purchase, but here comes the magic – when people are looking for something on Amazon, they are looking exclusively to buy something. Amazon has over 600 million credit cards in their database and this makes it unbeatable compared other platforms.

Kindle Direct Publishing (KDP) is an exclusive service from Amazon that allows *anyone* to self-publish his/her books and get money from them. I repeat – *Anyone* can publish a kindle eBook about any kind of niche. If you are wondering what this business requires, the answer is commitment, motivation, and good English skills.

You will tell yourself now that you are not a writer and you can't do something like that. You do not have to be a writer, you can hire someone to write the books for you, someone who uses your instructions and ideas. I'm sure you've seen a lot of fancy books on Amazon, a lot of them being written by famous authors and other books written by indie publishers (like you and I). You don't need to design an eBook cover for yourself, you can also hire a freelancer who can create a cover for you for $10.

You don't need to do all this by yourself, you need to hire people and outsource these tasks – you are an entrepreneur rather than a writer. I like to write my own books, but I like to give tasks such as proofreading, ghostwriting, or cover designing to others. I believe that my time is much more valuable than $10 for some tasks that may take more than 2 hours. Time is money, so be careful how you evaluate your time.

Chapter 2: How Does It Work?

Independently publish with Kindle Direct Publishing to reach millions of readers.

Get to market fast. Publishing takes less than 5 minutes and your book appears on Kindle stores worldwide within 24-48 hours.

Make more money. Earn up to 70% royalty on sales to customers in the US, Canada, UK, Germany, India, France, Italy, Spain, Japan, Brazil, Mexico, Australia and more. Enroll in KDP Select and earn more money through Kindle Unlimited and the Kindle Owners' Lending Library.

Keep control. Keep control of your rights and set your own list prices. Make changes to your books at any time.

Get started today! Publish your books with KDP. Learn how easy it is.

You just have to go to the www.kdp.amazon.com, create an account and complete all the required fields.

As soon as you finish completing all the fields, you can publish any book and however many books you want. You will now probably ask, "And what am I supposed to write about?" or "I'm not a writer, I can't do that." Oh, actually, yes, you can. Remember what I told you last chapter – *Anyone* can do it.

How? Here's the fun part – you have 2 big possibilities. You can write the book yourself, which I highly recommend in the beginning to make some cash and then to reinvest the money in hiring freelancers to help you out with all the time consuming tasks.

How much money can you earn?

It depends. You can earn $100 to $1,000,000 or even more. It depends on you, on what you want to publish, if you publish fiction or non-fiction books, the niches that you choose, on what markets you have, and also depends on the quality of the book and what you deliver to readers, if you give them the value you have promised in your title and description.

What should I write about to have success?

Write about whatever you like, but before you decide what to do, you should write about a topic that you already have knowledge about. The best books that you will create will be those about that which you have some knowledge about. If you know what you are talking about in a book, if you have experience and if you enjoy learning new things about that topic, then start writing.

Decide what you want to write about and then do *market research*.

Market research takes an hour or so to do and it's the most important part of your future success with KDP. If the topic that you have knowledge about also sells well on Amazon, then go ahead with it. In the next chapter, I will show you how to do market research properly.

Chapter 3: How to Do Market Research

This is the most important part of how you can make money on Kindle:

Let's see an example. You want to do some market research about... weight loss or diets. You need to go to "Kindle eBooks", then you choose the main category, which is "Health, Fitness and Dieting":

Show results for

Health, Fitness & Dieting

New Releases
Last 30 days (4,894)
Last 90 days (14,689)
Coming Soon (525)

‹ Kindle Store
‹ Kindle eBooks
Health, Fitness & Dieting
Alternative Medicine (17,814)
Beauty & Fashion (4,263)
Death & Grief (5,454)
Diets & Weight Loss (18,270)
Disorders & Diseases (13,869)
Exercise & Fitness (9,582)
Mental Health (14,989)
Nutrition (8,456)
Personal Health (23,272)
Psychology & Counseling (48,201)
Recovery (3,707)
Reference (967)
Relationships (28,831)
Safety & First Aid (1,076)
Sex (6,181)

Refine by

Author
J. J. Virgin (2)
Susan Cain (1)
Mike Dooley (1)
Daniel Kahneman (1)
Dale Carnegie (4)
Dallas Hartwig (2)
Melissa Hartwig (2)
▸ See more

Recommended for You

Diabetes Cure: My Against All Odds...
Jessica Brennan, William Black...
☆☆☆☆☆ (10)
Kindle Price: $10.53
Why recommended?

Paleo Diet: 365 Days of Paleo Diet...
▸ Emma Katie
☆☆☆☆☆ (5)
Kindle Price: $1.23
Why recommended?

▸ See more recommendations

Best-selling Books in Featured Categories

DAVE ASPREY

Diets & Weight Loss
The Bulletproof Diet: Lose...
Dave Asprey, J.J. Virgin
10-Day Green Smoothie...
JJ Smith
Wheat Belly Total Health...
William Davis

You cannot publish a book that outranks all the other books. You can obviously see that there are thousands of books for each subcategory, so what you want to do is to go deeper into the other subcategories.

< Kindle Store
< Kindle eBooks
< Health, Fitness & Dieting
Diets & Weight Loss
  Diets (17,512)
  Food Counters (1,003)
  Special Conditions (203)

We choose "Diets & Weight Loss" for the next subcategory and then we go further to "Diets" and then to "Weight Loss". Now there are no other many micro categories and notice that it is much easier to outrank 2,000 – 9,000 books than 200,000 or more.

< Kindle Store
< Kindle eBooks
< Health, Fitness & Dieting
< Diets & Weight Loss
< Diets
Weight Loss

You need to look for certain keywords that people are searching all the time.

Include those keywords in your description, title, and subtitle and when they are required (I will cover this later on).

We have found all of the subcategories, so now you look for titles that others have and sell. You need to know what is selling the most. You go to kindle books and choose "Best Seller" and then you look after the category and subcategories you have already chosen. You will see top 100 paid and top 100 free.

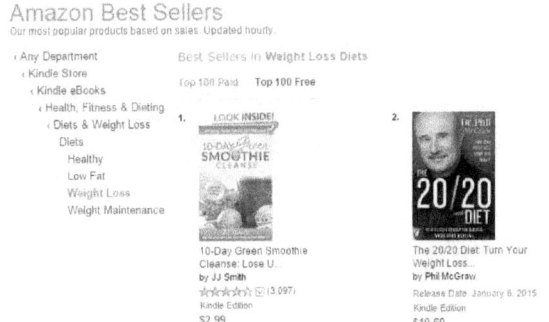

Then you want to click on some books and see what rank they have and how well are they selling these books with those titles.

Amazon Best Sellers Rank: #462 Paid in Kindle Store (See Top 100 Paid in Kindle Store)
  #1 in Kindle Store > Kindle eBooks > Health, Fitness & Dieting > Diets & Weight Loss > Diets > Weight Maintenance
  #1 in Kindle Store > Kindle eBooks > Health, Fitness & Dieting > Diets & Weight Loss > Diets > Weight Loss
  #1 in Kindle Store > Kindle eBooks > Health, Fitness & Dieting > Nutrition

Would you like to give feedback on images or tell us about a lower price?

Amazon Bestseller's Rank shows how many copies the author sold in that day. Now you will think...hmm, isn't 462 a big number? NO! In fact, it's too good to be real. The lower the rank, the better it is and more sales you have. This book is ranked #462 in the whole Kindle store and in the Kindle store, there are over 3,100,000 books.

Amazon helps you see everything and it does all the marketing for you. You don't have to know anything about marketing. The book shows you what is selling best, that means #1 for the Weight

Maintenance category, #1 for Weight Loss, and #1 for Nutrition. There is a kdpcalculator, which tells you how much you sell by rank. At rank #462 paid in Kindle store, you sell 100 to 300 copies a day.

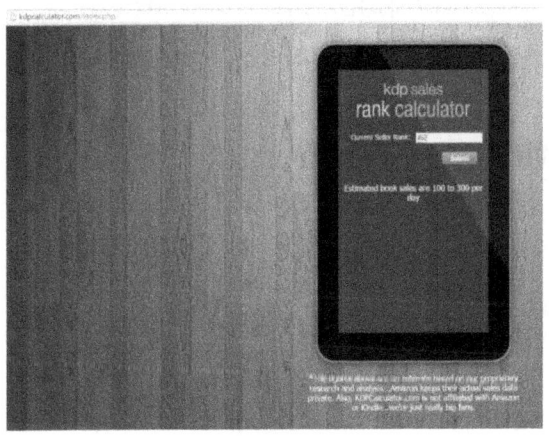

If you write a book in one of those Top Paid # subcategories, even if it's the last one, then congratulations, you are on your way to success.

So let's summarize:

1. Find out what topics you like.
2. You go to Kindle Store
3. You choose a niche
4. Choose category, subcategories, and micro categories
5. Do some market research, go to top #100 paid books in that category
6. Look for some titles and look at how good are they selling and figure out which is selling best
7. Find the best keywords in Amazon search bar and look at what market you have

Chapter 4: Starting Your Book

As soon as you finish doing market research and you choose a good and profitable niche, figure out a title, an eye catching title, a subtitle, with a lot of keywords. Do not make short titles like *Weight Loss Guide*. It's very bad, it doesn't suggest anything. Do something like *Extreme Weight Loss Bible – The Fastest Way to Lose Weight, Gain Your Health, and Live a Happy Life*.

I hope you got the idea. You include more keywords and it's easier to rank the book and it's even easier for buyers to find your book. The more keywords you have, the more readers you reach and the more money you make.

The book you want to write and make money with must have an original content, any copy from Google or other is plagiarism and you get into real trouble. So, make sure your book's content is 100% original. You can outsource it though, don't panic.

To sell a lot of books, create a lot of books, and make a lot of money, you need to focus on a few main things:

1. Books have to be short (15 – 80 pages), you can write longer ones, but you waste money and time.
2. You have to deliver what you have promised in the title (How to... swim... Well... teach them exactly how to swim)
3. Write a lot of these on the most profitable niches you find.
4. Repeat the first three.

Chapter 5: How Do I Write My Book?

You do not have to if you are not a writer. You may write the book by yourself if you want and you are good at writing, but be aware that an awful book with a lot of mistakes won't sell too much or for too long.

Where to go?

You have some options. You can go to http://freelancer.com but it's a little bit complicated, the fastest way and the best service, in my opinion, is http://iWriter.com

You can have books written for low prices, or if you want the ultimate quality content and you have money to invest, you can pay even more than $1,000 for a book.

Decide what chapters (titles) you want to add to your books, and give them to writers to write as articles, do not give them to write as a full length eBook. Why? They will charge you more!

If you want to write a book with 15 chapters (articles) with at least 1,000 words each, they will cost you $157.5 and you get 15,000–16,000 words, which is a book with 80-100 pages on Kindle (depending on the spacing, font size, if you have pictures, etc.)

Project type:	🔲	Have articles written ▼
Project description:	🔲	
Category:	🔲	-- select a category -- ▼
Article length:	🔲	1000 ▼
Article language:	🔲	English (US) ▼
Submit to:	🔲	⚪ **Basic** : All writers will see your request.
		⦿ **Premium** : 4.1 to 5 star writers will see your request.
		⚪ **Elite** : 4.6 to 5 star writers will see your request.
		⚪ **Elite Plus** : 4.85 to 5 star writers will see your request.
Price per article: 🔲		$0.00 (minimum $10.50 per article)
Keyword(s):	🔲	9
(Type each keyword on a new line)		10
		11
		12
		13
		14
		15
Total project cost:	🔲	$157.50

Now, to write an eBook with at least 7,000 words (mandatory), it requires you to pay at least $160. You pay even less for the previous method for which you get more than double in length.

Project type:		Have a Kindle book written	▼
Project description:			
Category:		Health and Fitness	▼
eBook length:		7.000 (~20 pages) ▼	
Article language:		English (US) ▼	
Submit to:		● **Premium** : 4.1 to 5 star writers will see your request.	
		○ **Elite** : 4.6 to 5 star writers will see your request.	
		○ **Elite Plus** : 4.85 to 5 star writers will see your request.	
Project price:		$0.00 (minimum $160.00 per article)	
Chapter titles:		● You choose the titles for the writer.	
		○ Allow writer to make up their own titles.	
Total chapters:		1 ▼	

Now, don't worry, you do not have to pay anything to writers until you like the content, you can ask them to rewrite everything until you are satisfied with it.

Okay, so you give them the chapters, the titles, the instructions, you get your book done within 2-10 days, depending on how hard your writer works and how much work he has to do.

Before we move on to the next chapters, let me tell you something – if you want to do an outstanding job on Kindle, you need to be sure that the book you are about to write will be high quality, and it will deliver value to readers. With these qualities + the right advertising methods, you will dominate the market very quickly.

Chapter 6: How to Make Your Cover

There are 3 main ways to design your cover:

1. Design it yourself – Use photo editing software (such as Adobe Photoshop, for example, any other software is okay as well). Select or buy a stock image from www.fotolia.com or www.shutterstock.com and insert it in your future cover. The aspect ratio that Amazon requires for eBook is 1.6 – so a cover with the resolution of 1600x1000 pixels should be perfect. If you don't know Photoshop, you can learn it in a couple of months or you can use the next two alternative methods. If you are planning to design a cover that can also be used for CreateSpace, use a 6 x 9

inches format in Adobe Photoshop and select 300 dpi level.

2. Use Cover Creator within Amazon – it's free and easy to use. You have to put in a title, the author's name, and an image/background color. When you choose to do this, the cover that you create will be instantly uploaded.

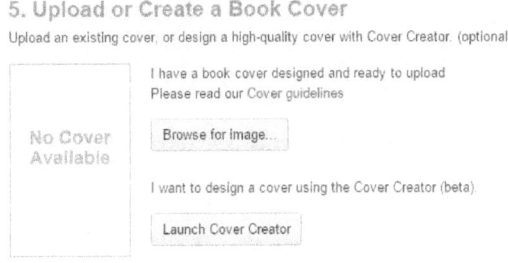

3. Pay for your cover – You have multiple solutions (multiple websites and different levels of quality). You can have your book designed on www.99designs.com by premium designers. An eBook cover is $299 to $1,199 (from bronze to platinum level

designers – $299 bronze, $499 silver, $799 gold, or $1,199 platinum). You just tell them what you want in your cover, what they should follow, and you will get 30 to 90 premium designs from which you choose only one (it's a contest based design – a lot of designers enter the contest and you choose the best design).

You can also have your cover created on www.freelancer.com or other freelancing websites for a similar price.

If you want a really cheap cover that will be ready in less than 24 hours, go on www.fiverr.com and you will find a lot of designers there who make really nice designs for the money you pay. I usually pay $10-$20 for my cover on Fiverr and I get it done within 3 days. Some of the covers from my books are made by myself (these book covers are made by me).

I recommend you let the guys from http://Fiverr.com do that for you for only $5 (or $10-20 if you have any premium requirements). You get it 24 hours to 3 days later, depending how many people are in queue.

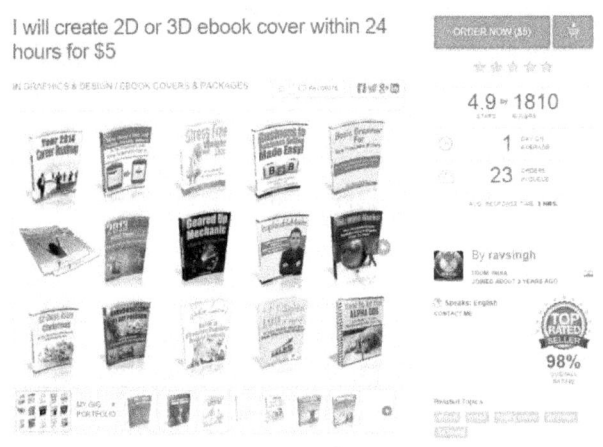

I worked with designers from Fiverr. They deliver the covers fast and you don't have to do any additional tasks.

Let them do them for you, I think $5 or so isn't worth the time to design the cover yourself and lose precious hours. If you don't have the money, or you want to use that money to promote your book, then do it yourself.

Chapter 7: Formatting the Book

As soon as you choose your niche and you do market research (see previous chapters), you can start writing your book. Use Microsoft Word for Windows or Pages for Mac OS.

Make sure to write an introduction, good quality content, a conclusion, and most important of all, a table of contents (TOC).

It's important to create a table of contents, as readers shouldn't have to scroll all the time to go to a specific chapter of a book because that would be really annoying for them. It's easy to do it, you just need to insert Bookmarks and Hyperlinks to the Bookmarks you create; there are a lot of tutorials on YouTube on how to do it. There are just

3 buttons to use – Insert -> Bookmark and Hyperlink (in Microsoft Word).

If you aren't too good at formatting a book or you do not want to waste time, you can go to www.Fiverr.com and let the guys format it and proofread your work (which somebody else did as well) for $5 or $10.

Make sure your content is clean. It provides valuable information to the readers and ensures you do not have any grammatical mistakes. Spelling mistakes are bad in any book and they must be avoided as much as possible even though there's no book in this world that doesn't have at least one mistake.

When you finish writing and formatting your book, you only have to upload it on Kindle and it will be automatically converted into the Kindle format from your .doc (Microsoft Word document format) or Pages format in just a couple of moments (it may take longer if you have pictures or such).

Chapter 8: Uploading Your Book

Now that you are done with your cover and content and you have formatted your book, you can upload it on Kindle.

Make sure you have an account. If you don't, sign up and let's get started. Before you can upload a book, you need to complete the tax information and make sure you have a credit card attached to the account. Unless you have these, you won't be able to continue to publish a book.

You go to www.kdp.amazon.com and then you go to your Bookshelf and click on "Add New Title". Now, what you have to do:
Tick the box with "Enroll in KDP Select".

KDP Select has two things to offer: Promotional free days (5 days every 90 days) for your book and also countdown deals and Kindle Unlimited, which offers users the ability to borrow your books for a limited period of time, for free. The good thing is that you receive a small sum, Amazon has a monthly fund for the whole number of books that are borrowed each month and depending on how many books you lend, the more you will get.

So make sure to tick that box.

Next, you enter your title, subtitle, you as an author. Use pen names, look for the most suitable pen names for the type of niche that you are posting in. Another important aspect is not to combine a lot of different niches for one pen name.

For example, choose a name like James Rodes for a health niche and John Taylor for a business niche. You are the publisher, the authors are the pen names you choose. It's indicated by Amazon to do so and not to confuse people.
"Hey, what am I buying here, a cookbook from an author who sells engineering books?"
 It doesn't go well. So choose a pen name for every niche. (a general one, I hope you've got the point)

Choose your language (the language of the content from the book, probably English, but you can write in any language) and then tick below the "This is not a public domain" box. That means you have an original content that isn't someone else's work.

Now add the categories, the ones for which you have done the market research (they will be a little different here than the ones on the home page, choose the ones that are the closest to ones on the home page)

Upload your cover and then your content. As soon as you upload, it will tell you if you have spelling mistakes and it will tell you where you do if you have any. It may take longer to upload if you have images in your book content.

Then you click "Save and Continue" down below and move to the next one.

Then you choose the royalty options, which are 35% and 70% - you receive 35%. You can put a price between $0 and $200, but the range between $2.99 and $9.99 gets 70% royalty. In the beginning, you will choose $0.99 and I will explain why in the following chapter.

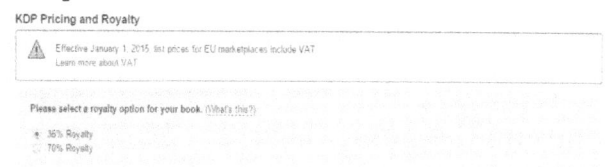

Chapter 9: Promoting Your Book and Getting Your First Sales

Here's where you will be nervous and you can't wait to see some money coming from your book. I will honestly tell you that it takes two weeks to a month until you start making money passively and continuously, each month.

What you have to do:

Ask your family, friends, pay someone, or just wait to get some reviews. Your first reviews matter a lot to your book. As soon as you get between 5 and 10 reviews, you can go to your KDP account to KDP Select and set 1 to 5 days to make your book free (I recommend at least 3) – you will get a minimum of 50-100 downloads/day so for 3 days, you should get a minimum of 150-400 downloads (without any paid promotions).

Now, here's a small problem – that number of downloads isn't enough to make daily sales. You need to invest in advertising and there are hundreds of methods which I discussed in my second book, which is about how to promote your book.

http://www.amazon.com/Kindle-Publishing-Unveiled-Advertise-marketing-ebook/dp/B00RUAWW72/ref=sr_1_2?s=digital-text&ie=UTF8&qid=1422110873&sr=1-2&keywords=kindle+publishing+unveiled&pebp=1422110877570&peasin=B00RUAWW72

From those downloads, you may get some reviews, and from those downloads, you rank higher and will start to appear in Amazon's searches and people will start finding your book more easily, even when you are done with the free promotion days.

As soon as you finish this, your book is on autopilot for three months; it will generate passive income. Every three months, you need to promote your book again and to update it (if necessary). You will be surprised to see $10/month to up to $1,000/month or even more, depending on the niche, market, audience, and how well you advertise your book.

Advertising is crucial for any kind of product you want to sell – quality is also essential for long-term profits, but in the short-term, advertising is what will boost your sales and rankings. What I'm saying is try to combine quality with advertising and you will be surprised by the results.

There are a lot more details to cover here but I will present the basics and what you have to do ASAP to make money.

Join Twitter and Facebook groups, put links with your free book, and go to sites that host your book when it's free and boost your downloads on the free promotion trial. If you have a blog, website, or YouTube channel, use them to promote your book.

There are websites that charge $10 to $500 for one book, but they have proved to be highly effective. It's not wise to invest $500 in one single website. I like to go to different websites and invest around $150-$200 in 4-5 websites.

Chapter 10: Getting Paid

Everyone is very excited when they are releasing their first book or their first books. You won't see any sales in the first 2-3 weeks, so be patient. There's a whole process to do before that. It's natural not to receive any money in your first days and weeks because you are nowhere to find on Amazon; your book just got there and needs some attention.

If the book is good and someone is looking for that specific topic, you may sell your book without any reviews or without any advertising, but this happens very rarely.

If you do as I recommended in the previous chapters, to do market research, write your book, make a good cover, format your book, publish it, and choose good keywords, *then* what will really boost and send your book on the sales track will be to use the KDP Select free days and try to a minimum promotion on websites, Facebook groups, Fiverr, etc., to make additional downloads.

The more downloads you get, the higher you will rank for your title and keywords, and your book will show up higher in the searches. That's what you need, and sales will start to come after a month (of publishing).

The free promotion days can boost your sales for one book up to 500% and you are allowed to use 5 days every 90 days in KDP Select, so use them wisely.

How and when are you going to get paid by Amazon?

You will get paid every 60 days - Amazon sends you an email 10 days before the payment is processed (generally on the 20th every month) and you will receive the money at the end of the month or the start of the new month – 29th to 2nd (next month).

Tip – the money you earn from borrows (KOLL/KU units) are also paid on the same date, but you will see the reports for borrows in the "Prior Month Royalties" – Amazon sends you a report on 15th for the previous month and it will show you how much money you made from everything including borrows.

You will usually get from $1.35 to $1.5 for a borrow, depending on the number of borrows in total for that month. Notice that you will have a paid borrow if a customer who borrows your book has read at least 10% of the book. If a customer doesn't read at least 10%, you won't get paid (usually, almost all of the borrows are paid).

UPDATE 1st July 2015

The KU/KOLL system has been changed as a result of complaints of authors and I totally agree with the new system. Instead of being paid if at least 10% of your book is read, authors are now paid for every individual page that was read.

What does this mean? If you have a 20 page book, you will get paid for those 20 pages that a customer reads. If you are unlucky and the customer doesn't like your book, he/she will borrow your book, read 2 pages, and throw it away.

Before this update, everyone earned $1.35 for a borrow, no matter how long the book was. Now, a 20 page book will earn $0.2 (if fully read) if the price per page is $0.01. Similarly, if an author has a novel that has 500 pages, the author will earn $5 for a borrow (if the book is fully read).

In conclusion, writers who have less than 135 pages will earn less than before, writers who have 135 pages will earn the same, and writers who have lengthy books will earn more.

The number of pages will be calculated automatically by KENP (Kindle Edition Normalized Pages), so don't try to fool the system with big fonts and double spacing because it won't work.

Chapter 11: The Six Figure Recipe – Myth or Reality?

Now, I've presented how to write, publish, design, and promote your book. Now we are interested in getting a 6 figure annual passive income, aren't we?

A book (usually) generates $50 to $500, depending on a lot of factors (niche, content, title, value, number of pages, price, etc.). Now, think – how many books do you need and how much time does it take to reach over $100,000/year?

Here is the answer:

Write one book a month – Spend time working on your book each day. In the two weeks, write it yourself or get content for your book, arrange all your ideas, and create the content. During the 3rd week, focus on polishing the details of your book – proofread, cover, formatting, and other minor details. In the 4th week, make sure to promote it.

If you do all of these properly, you will be able to generate at least $200 from a single book, every single month, but be sure to promote it again every three months. To grow this Kindle Publishing business, you need to permanently improve yourself, your books, and to invest money.

Now, you will not have the same results for each book. You will have one that makes $1,000/month, two that make $50/month, and five that make $200/month – you will ever know exactly how much money you will make and every month is different (regarding sales). If you create one book a month and you make in average $300/book, in one year, you will be able to generate around $3,600/month, after two years, $7,200, and after three years, $10,800/month.

You will never be able to reach these numbers without a blog, a YouTube channel, paid advertising, and a *lot* of work on a daily basis. Anyone who tells you that being an online entrepreneur, an author, or a freelancer is easy doesn't know what they're talking about. The only things what make this business very attractive are:

1. It is scalable – You control it and you can grow it without any limits.
2. You obtain profits very quickly – This is probably the fastest method to make money online (as far as I'm concerned,

it's the fastest method I personally know).

Okay, so after three years of hard work, you will be able to generate $10,800, but you won't get $10,800 net profit. You will be paying a withholding tax from 10 to 30% (depending on if you are a resident of U.S. or non-U.S. resident), you will need to invest at least 20% of the money you earn (advertising, content, blog, virtual assistant, etc.). Out of $10,800, which is $129,600 gross income, from which you pay 15% as a U.S. resident, 30% as a non-U.S. resident, or 10% if you are a non-U.S. resident but the country in which you live is in tax treaties with U.S. (my case). This is available only for sales made in the U.S. store (which are 80-90% of your total sales). In the other stores, you don't pay any withholding taxes, but you pay VAT (for EU).

Let's say you pay 15%, for 85% of that $129,600 – you will need to pay 15% tax for $110,160, which is $16,524. Y + our total amount of money remaining is ($110,160 – $16,524 + $19,440 (sales made on the other stores for which withholding taxes are not applied) so you will be making $113,076 net income, but you need to invest at least 20% in advertising and other services to grow and maintain your income – $22,615. So your final remaining amount of money per year after three years of hard work will be $90,480. If you push hard one more year, you will exceed $100,000 per year net income, but you need to be very serious with yourself and you need to be dedicated to this business.

If you are lucky enough, you will probably reach those number faster, but I believe that no matter what you do, as an indie publisher, you won't be able to reach a 6 figure annual income in less than 2 years. This isn't a 'get rich scheme', it's a business that requires work and dedication.

You just manage all these tasks and tell other people what to do for you. A freelancer creates a cover, another one creates the content, and another one promotes it. You just take everything and put them all together and wait for your sales to come by.

The only condition here is if you really want to achieve this goal. Even if it sounds easy, it isn't that easy, but it's a lot easier than other ways to make money.

Conclusion

Kindle is a gold mine and there are few people who know about this. It's continually evolving all over the world as people are now consuming a lot more information online and on their tablets, laptops, PCs, smartphones. And, it's natural to do so, it's more efficient, it's a lot faster, and you can keep with you on the go, providing unlimited content on your tablet. An eBook has less than 1-2 MB size. If you don't agree, please go ahead and carry 10-15 pounds of paper in your backpack.

It's a lot faster. You do not deliver the book from USA to Europe or vice-versa, you just click buy or download and it's delivered almost instantly. No more taxes, no more killed trees, no more high taxes and commissions. This is the future, the future is *digital* and it expands in that way. Old paper books will become history a few years from now.

If this book has been useful to you, please be kind and write a short review about what you think, I would be more than grateful if you want to share your thoughts with me.

Thank you